You Are
Worth
Millions

You just don't know it.

William Medina

ISBN: 1484027493
ISBN-13: 978-1484027493

DEDICATION

This book is dedicated to my two children Keira and Isaac. They continue to be my inspiration. As I seek to teach them, I myself strive to learn more, to accomplish more. It is by the grace of God that I and my wife have such wonderful children.

ACKNOWLEDGMENTS

I would like to acknowledge my wife Magda, my daughter Keira and my son Isaac. They have all in their individual ways have been inspirational in helping me write this book.

Foreword

"You is kind. You is smart. You is important."
~Aibileen Clark

From the book: The Help, authored by Kathryn Stockett

I love this phrase, I admit I never read the book but I did see the movie. When I saw the scene where Aibileen Clark (Viola Davis) held the little girl on her lap and told her that she was kind, smart and important – it hit a cord deep inside me. It brought to mind all the times my mother looked me in the eyes with this intense look and told me that I was special, that I had worth. While many around me were saying I was worthless, a poor beggar, that there was nothing special about me – she would remind me that I was important.

You is kind.
You is Smart.
You is important.

It's not proper grammar and does not lend itself to style or dramatic flair – but it is powerful.

I grew up in poverty, through many trials and tragedies. I lived in poverty stricken neighborhoods surrounded by many whose only relief from poverty was found in making others feel small, weak, and worthless. But I was always able to keep moving forward because I had my mother, a single mother of seven children who reminded each one of us that we were special, that we were important, and yes, that we should be kind.

I also thank God for the many other people who crossed my path in life, people who took the time to tell me that I had talent, I had potential, I was worthy of respect because I had worth. Even total strangers like one such older gentleman who walking by me on the street one day, paused to tell an insecure boy who was walking with his head down in an attempt to avoid people as he was walking alone in a very dangerous neighborhood — as he passed by me he said "you are a man, hold your head up high like one". Those simple few words still ring loudly in my heart today.

In today's society people are looked upon as numbers, as cattle or as sheep. It seems as if everyone is simply looking to take advantage of someone else, to take advantage of you. We have the slogans and the promotions "everyone is special in their own way". But it doesn't resonant in our hearts and minds because it's just that a slogan, a fancy catch phrase that is thrown around to make people feel good about themselves but does nothing else.

I wrote this book "You are worth Millions" not because I know that you have special talents or because I want you to feel good – but because I literally mean it. You are worth millions, you don't know it – so chances are you will most likely mess it up for yourself.

Most young adults struggle with self worth, self appreciation and yes so do adults. But it seems to hit teens in an adverse way because after all, they are just starting out in life, they know little about themselves and even less about the world. The sad thing is that the young people of our generation do not realize how much potential they have – the opportunities that lay before them.

I am not going to pretend that I know without a shadow of a doubt that you have special talents that will propel you to greatness in life. Nor will I say that you are destined for success because you have a "special" gift. In truth, if anything, television programs like the Voice, American Idol and the sort should help young people today understand that there are hundreds of thousands of very talented people out there – all wanting success and a better life. What I can say with absolute assurance is that everyone has the same opportunity to succeed. In fact even people in the most dire of straights can achieve what I am offering to you this day. I am not offering you some secret formula for success, but rather helping you realize that everything you need for success will be put into your hands – what you do with it is all up to you.

That's been one of my mantras - focus and simplicity. Simple can be harder than complex: You have to work hard to get your thinking clean to make it simple. But it's worth it in the end because once you get there, you can move mountains.

~ Steve Jobs

YOU ARE WORTH MILLIONS
I CAN PROVE IT

Let me start with this one clear statement that I believe always needs repeating:

You are worth Millions!

With that said let me make this clear – this is not a feel good, you are special, believe it and you can achieve it kind of guru self help (pixie dust) statement. This is cold honest factual truth that most people and especially young people do not know, or much less have been informed about.

It is an undeniable absolute fact, you are worth millions – you just don't know it. And because you do not know or understand this to be truth, you will most likely mess it all up for yourself.

Let it sink in and repeat it to yourself: you are, better yet say – "I am worth millions".

You are, you are worth millions and everyone knows this, except for you. It doesn't matter where you are, who you are, what side of the street or train tracks you are from – you are worth millions.

How can I say this? It's simple, because it's true.

Now, I've said it enough times hopefully that it has at minimum sunk into your brain just enough to peak your interest. So now let me take some much needed time to prove this to you.

Proving you're worth Millions.

As I stated before this is not about making you feel good – good feelings will not help you. Good feelings can be overrun by bad feelings, hurt feelings, negative thoughts and the surmounting crowds of nay Sayers that seek only to belittle you.

The world is full of people that only feel good when they make you feel bad – in essence, they feel powerful, successful when they make you feel small, cheap and worthless. The world is also full of people who know you have worth and they desire your worth. As I would put it – they know you have worth (worth millions) and they want to benefit or profit from you.

The problem is we are often surrounded by those who want to drag us down, put us down and drain us of our self worth because it suits their needs. For many years I had a very good friend who I loved like a brother, I had three 'blood relative' brothers but to me, he was my brother. But our relationship had one minor problem: He had low self esteem issues and he used me to make himself feel important. In order for him to feel good, he had to tear me down. He simply could not stand to see me succeed because that meant he had to face his issues with his insecurity.

It took several years for me to break ties with my close friend and I was only able to do so because someone pointed out to me, in a clear understandable way; that I was worth more than what I thought I was. When I finally came around to understanding what they meant, that I am valuable, I am worth something and therefore should consider myself as such – I could no longer continue to be his friend. I could no longer allow him to belittle me, to abuse our friendship, to mock me so that he could feel better about himself.

This is why I love this quote:

When your self-worth goes up, your net worth goes up with it.
~Mark Victor Hansen

When you understand that you are worth something. That you are worth more than what other people say you are, believe you are – something changes inside of you and soon that change comes out to shine.

You are worth millions. Maybe not today, not tomorrow but you are worth millions. And like my friend who took advantage of our friendship to put me down in order to prop himself up, to make himself feel better about himself. If you are not careful, people will be taking advantage of you as well. People who do not understand their worth – are often very easily taken advantage of.

How do I know you are worth Millions?

Remember, as I said this is not intended to be a make you feel good or a make you feel special statement. I am not here to tell you that you are one of a kind and that there is no one else in the world like you. While it is true that you are one of a kind, that in itself will not help you get ahead in life. The truth is – there are a million or more people walking the earth that are just like you.

Again, I am not saying that you are not unique, different, a one of a kind individual – what I am saying is that there are millions of people with the same opportunity and the same circumstance.

As unique as you can be, we all have one common factor: the average person will live to reach the age of 70. Not everyone, but on average – the life expectancy of the average American is 70. Of those 70 years it is estimated that if you deduct your years as a child, young adult life and the years you spend as a retiree – the average person will have worked a total of 43 years.

Makes you wonder doesn't? More than half your life is spent working, by working I mean as in a job, a career or a business. Forty three years working, Monday thru Friday, some Saturdays and Sundays with maybe a two week vacation if you are lucky. Makes me kind of wonder why some children are in such a rush to grow up? If they really knew what was waiting for them, they would enjoy their lazy afternoons and long summer breaks a lot more.

So now that we know that half a person's life (an estimated 43 years) is spent working. How do I go about proving that you are worth millions – literally speaking?

We know that the average person lives to be roughly 70 years old. Out of those 70 years the average person works 43 of these years. So if we apply a bit of math we can come up with the 'life time earnings' of an individual.

For instance: If we calculate that after some college the average person starts "working" at age 22 and has a modest annual income of $10,000 dollars a year with a 1% annual increase to that income, when they retire (age 65) they would have earned about $550,000 dollars.

43 years X income ($10,000 with 1% increase yearly) = $533,978 [earned over life time – years worked]

Don't believe me – do the math.

Or you can go online and do a search for: earn over life time calculator

I researched this information on a financial calculator I found at: http://www.calcxml.com/do/ins07

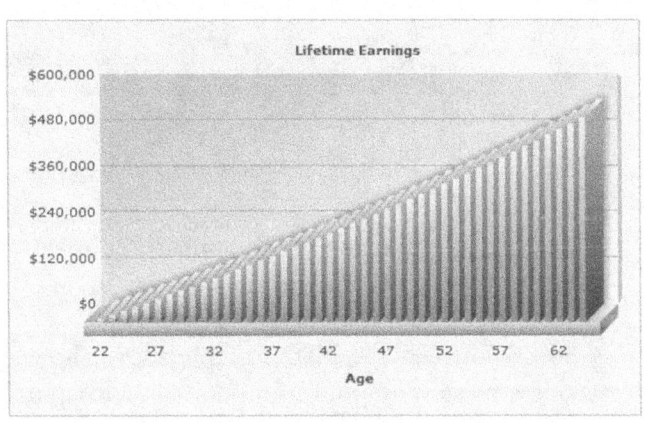

The chart above states: Based on your current

earnings it appears that you will earn $533,978 over the next 43 years.

It doesn't sound like a lot but when was the last time you held half a million dollars in your hands?

But let's not stop there, what about a person who earns $20,000 dollars a year? How much would they have earned over a life time?

start working @ 22, retire @ 65 earning $20K a yr w/ 1% annual increase

Results

Based on your current earnings it appears that you will earn $1,067,956 over the next 43 years.

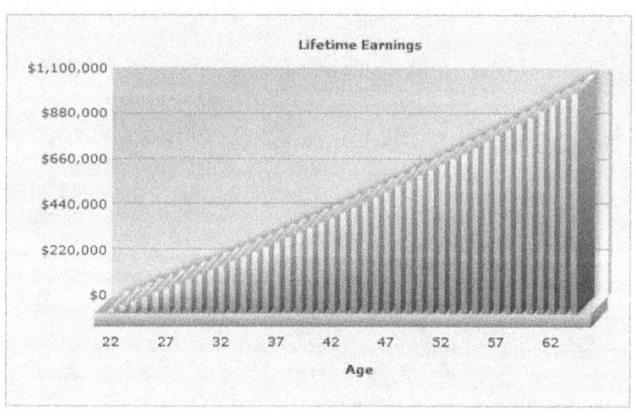

Making $20,000 a year with an annual 1% increase for 43 years totals $1,067,956 dollars – Wow!

So as you can see in the graph above, how even making a modest amount of money can add up to be a large sum over a life time of work. It's important that you understand this in order for you to see how valuable you truly are: You are worth millions.

I am sure you have heard it said before, people who have said "If I only had a million dollars". They usually go on to say that having that amount of money would drastically change their lives forever. That if they had this money they would do things differently. But the truth is – most people have a million dollars or they will earn more than a million dollars in their life time.

You have to ask yourself – what are they doing with that?

It is not proven or set in stone, but the magic number given as the number (amount income) to be considered middle class is somewhere between $35,000 and $100,000. Some have even lowered that range to be between $19,000 and $91,000 in annual income. For most Americans like me – we have been lead to believe that a $50,000 annual income is the starting point for the middle class. For the sake of avoiding a long discussion; for the purpose of this book I am just going to go with $50,000 a year for a single person, this will classify them as middle class.

Now with that said, would you agree that $50,000 dollars a year is a lot of money? Most people would say yes, especially for a single person to live on. So what I am going to do is I am going to lower that down to $40,000 a year to see how much an individual would earn over a life time (43 working years) with no annual raise – just a flat yearly income.

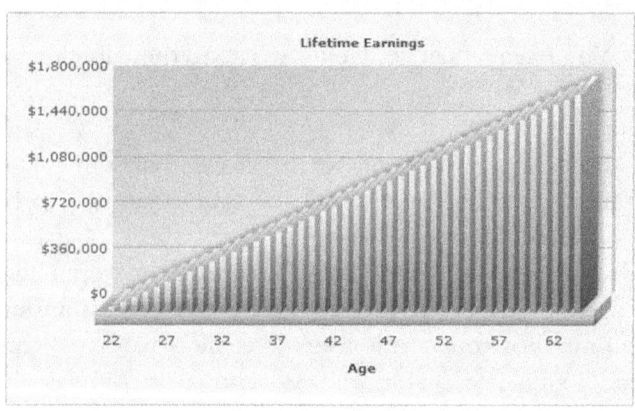

Earnings and Assumptions	
Current age	22
Retirement age	65
Current annual income ($)	40000
Annual salary increases: (%)	0%

Results

Based on your current earnings it appears that you will earn $1,720,000 over the next 43 years.

As you can see in the previous chart, an individual earning $40,000 dollars a year for 43 years and with no annual raise – will have earned $1,720,000 dollars. Now that is a lot of money!

Using this financial calculator I can prove to you that you are worth millions.

Over the course of your life, you have the potential to make millions – therefore you are worth millions.

You don't believe me?

You don't have to believe me. I am 100% sure that you will want to eat. You will want to have a place to live in. You will want to dine out, go to the theater, and take trips on occasion. All these things and many more will require money – money you earn by working. And whether you believe that you are worth millions or not – every company, every business, every local, state and federal government knows, you are worth millions to them.

Every company in the world tries to make money by selling you products and services. Why, because they want your money. You make it, you earned it and they want it. In fact, these same companies spend thousands if not millions of dollars trying to figure out what you might be interested in purchasing.

Companies make millions telling other companies what will sell in a particular demographic.

Demographics: Demographics are statistical data about the characteristics of a population, such as the age, gender and income of the people within the population.

Demographic profiles in marketing: Marketers typically combine several variables to define a demographic profile. A demographic profile (often shortened to "a demographic") provides enough information about the typical member of this group to create a mental picture of this hypothetical aggregate. For example, a marketer might speak of the single, female, middle-class, age 18 to 24, college educated demographic.

Researchers typically have two objectives in this regard: first to determine what segments or subgroups exist in the overall population; and secondly to create a clear and complete picture of the characteristics of a typical member of each of these segments. Once these profiles are constructed, they can be used to develop a "marketing strategy" and "marketing plan". The five types of demographics for marketing are age, gender, income level, race and ethnicity.

(www.yourdictionary.com/)

Basically they separate people into groups by age, sex, region, income, interest (such as likes & dislikes) and other characteristics to better have a feel for who would be interested in a particular product or service they plan to sell to the masses - which is you and me.

So while you may have difficulty believing that you are worth millions, businesses, corporations and others certainly understand how to profit from you – from your worth.

After all, why would they be so interested in you if you were not worth something to them? Again I say: you are worth millions. They know this, they understand this and they plan on you ignoring this fact.

If you took the time to learn about business you would see how different business, especially how large corporations think. They think in terms of years not weeks or months. Yes, you may hear of popular public companies that have stock holders to report to, speak in terms of quarterly reports (a report given every 3 months). But in essence, the report is to satisfy the individual stock holder who only thinks in terms of weeks and months.

Let me give you a simple illustration. Have you ever heard a bank commercial that said something to the effect of "You can trust us; we've been in business for 100 years….."

Businesses think long term. This is why when people want to start a business and go to the bank for a business loan – the bank wants to know what their business plan is for the next 2 to 5 years. The bank wants to know who you plan to sell to, as in 'demographics'.

The Bottom line

Let's face it, the bottom line is that you will work an 'x' amount of years to support yourself and at the end of that time span; you would (will) have earned an estimated $1.2 million dollars or possibly even more.

How much are you worth?

You are worth millions, the questions is – what will you do with it?

"Every individual has a place to fill in the world, and is important, in some respect, whether he chooses to be so or not."
~ Nathaniel Hawthorne

YOU ARE WORTH MILLIONS
TAKING ADVANTAGE

You are worth millions! As I have already proven to you in the previous chapter, you are worth millions. Granted it is over a life time or it can be done in a relative short period of time such as 30 years, 20 years and even as short as 10 or 5 years. The point being you are worth millions and people, businesses and companies know this. Even the government knows this - why do you think they tax you?

Now, the argument is that these millions you create over a life time is not worth much to you; notice they never say to the business' that want your money. They say that it doesn't help you to think about how much money you make over a life time because you have to factor in living expenses and taxes. While this is true, that the money 'You' earn over your life time is a large sum of money and yes - because of living expenses, taxes and other personal factors, you fail to keep much of that hard earned cash. I believe their argument is flawed, it's wrong.

Why do I believe that the argument is wrong, that how much money you make, as in millions, doesn't matter because you spend most of it on living? It's wrong because the arguments only strength is in the subtle belief that you cannot control 'how much money you keep'. And that is where I believe they are 100% wrong.

The last time I checked you are in control of how you make your money and most importantly - how you spend your money.

Now granted, you cannot save all the money you earn. You need to eat, dress yourself, you may need a car, and you most definitely need a place to live in, be it an apartment or a house. The fact is 'You' have to spend money in order to live and survive – that is how our society works.

Don't get me wrong, there are people who break the rules, they are the exception to societies standards: Like Mr. Daniel James Shellabarger who prefers to live in the desert with none of societies amenities.

Mr.Shellabarger, better known as 'Daniel Suelo' lives in the desert in a Utah cave. In 2009 he decided to stop using money – cold turkey, no cash at all. Of course he neither works, owns a car or owns a home and while he lives off the land, he occasionally enjoys the help [as in food, medical needs and bathing facilities] provided by friends whenever possible.

Yes, it can be done – you can live without the constraints of this society. But ask yourself this one question: how far will you go? Will you be happy living in the wild, in the desert, without a bathroom – or toilet tissue? I am sure most young men may say that they could do without the occasional shower but are you prepared to sleep on the floor knowing a snake, a spider; anything could crawl up beside you while you sleep?

Let's face it, 98 % of all Americans, – make that 98% of all the population in the world could not live without the amenities they have become accustomed to having in their everyday lives.

So you have to spend to live. You have to work in order to have money to spend and you have to spend money on the things you need for everyday life. But you forget, it is not the government, the business or the corporations who control you're spending habits – that is all you. You control how much money you spend. You also control how much money you save and invest for the future. So while yes you can earn millions over your life time and yes you have to spend some of that in order to live – you decide and you control how you spend it.

So while the argument is, you keep very little of the money you earn in your pocket, the response should be – I should work on keeping as much as I can since I earned it.

Everyone is after your Millions

You are worth at minimum about 1.2 million dollars over a life time. Reading it like this may not help you grasp the power of this statement so let me write it all out.

You are worth, at minimum $1,200,000 dollars over your life time.

And since you are worth this large amount of money you are a target, continuously pursued by every other person or entity in the world that wants your money. These entities, be it business, corporations, government, people or person – they are out there looking for ways to take your money. To them you are just a number, just a dollar sign they want to acquire.

As I stated earlier, businesses use 'Demographics' in order to make decisions on what products they should consider to sell to the public at large that have a high probability of selling well. They need and they want to make money. They need to make money for their investors, the owners, money to pay their employees – they need money. How do they make this money? They make it by taking it from you – excuse me, I mean selling you services and products.

It simply doesn't matter to these entities whether

you need the service and/or product. Or even if they have to manipulate you into 'believing' you need it (create desire, better known as creating a demand that was not there before) they simply want to know using demographics what is the best 'chance' they have of separating you from your money. As I like to call it, convincing you to willingly give them, your hard earned cash.

Let me give you a few examples of what I mean.

Everyone needs something to cover their feet, be it a pair of sneakers or shoes; you need something to protect your feet. So you 'need' to cover your feet – but do you purchase a pair of basic 'no name brand' sneakers that cost $29.99 or do you purchase a pair of $199.99 Nike sneakers said to be designed and used by a famous professional basketball player, so you can run faster and jump higher?

Choose: $29.99 to cover and protect my feet or $199.99 to cover and protect my feet?

It sounds silly when you look at it this way but people have been convinced, in fact millions of people have been convinced that they 'NEED' that pair of $199.99 Nike sneakers. It doesn't make them run faster. It doesn't make them jump any higher. It probably wasn't even designed by that professional basketball player – but people are convinced they need that sneaker.

As the saying goes:

"A foole and his monie be soone at debate, which after with sorrow repents him too late."
~ Thomas Tusser

That is an early version of the proverb: "A fool and his money are soon parted."

Are after your Millions

You may think that this is crazy to say – but even when a company seems to be doing 'Good', in truth they are only looking out for their bottom line (trying to get more money). Take for instance this bit of news I read about on January 15, 2013.

Can Bieber make prepaid cards cool?

"Justin Bieber recently made the leap into the financial-services world, endorsing a prepaid debit card."

The article mentions: That these 'pre-paid debit card' programs all speak to the same idea, teens spend way too much money. In fact it is said they spend to the tune of $200 billion dollars annually, according to researcher EPM Communications. Therefore this is a 'good way' for parents to be able to place curbs on all that buying & spending.

"A prepaid card can help since purchases are

limited to whatever dollar amount parents choose to put on the plastic."

It sounds like a great idea. What parent doesn't want to control their child's 'out of control' spending – to teach them how to manage money? But then the article goes on to state:

"Financial institutions have their own reasons for pushing prepaid, including recent federal legislation that limits in some cases what fees they can earn from traditional debit cards—but not from prepaid ones."

Article: Can Bieber make prepaid cards cool?
By Charles Passy, an article on MarketWatch.com

So I ask you:

If it is such a good idea to help parents curb their children's excessive spending habits.

Why do they need a Justin Bieber debit card?

Just my own assumption but: Could it be this particular company wants to capitalize on Justine Bieber's fan base, to grab hold of the millions of "tweens" that have Bieber fever? Let's not also fail to mention that the debit card company will charge parents (the expenses associated with prepaid cards), a monthly maintenance charge (as high as $10) to ATM fees (up to $2.50) all in an attempt to help Mom and Dad help teach their children how to better manage money.

So even while they say that they want to help, in truth – all you have to do is follow the money to see what they really want. This is to say more money (your money).

This is not to say that all companies are bad and that there are no companies left in the world that are doing good, that desires to do good in the world. Yes, there are many companies that seek to do good, to help, that have honest good intentions - but ultimately a business is a business and it needs to 'make money' in order to stay in business.

What I am trying to point out is that, you are worth at minimum $1.2 million dollars over a life time. You should be aware of the fact that there are hundreds if not thousands of people, business, corporations and even the government that have one specific goal in mind – separating you from your money.

It is very easy to say that it's hard to save money, but the truth is you can say the same about how hard it was for you to earn that money. Think of it, it will take you about 43 long hard working years, not counting teen age years or retirement, to earn $1.2 million dollars. But because you only see it in small increments over a life time – you think nothing of it as you spend it. Now imagine if you will, if I put a large mountain of money totaling $1.2 million dollars right in front of you: if I told you to burn half of that money, or to simply throw it out. Would you do it? Probably not, it's more likely you would think I was crazy. In fact you would justify me being crazy by simply saying "that this is a lot of money you're asking me to simply throw away, to squander".

Yet when we look at a $50 bill, a $20, or a $5 dollar bill we think nothing of it. We have no problem squandering it, spending it and even giving it away if need be. Why is this, we do it because in our mind we have been programmed to see it as 'it is only' one dollar or it's only five dollars, it's not a big deal – but it is.

Think of it as a drop of water. One drop of water falling on your head has little to no effect on you. It certainly can do no long lasting damage to you right? But what if I strapped you down and continuously dropped a single droplet of water onto your forehead, what would happen then?

What would happen is that the seemingly harmless droplet of water would drive you insane.

That is what is happening to millions of people every day across America. They are being driven insane, not by drops of water, but of their ever consuming debt. Debt they willingly accepted and they willingly asked for. They 'needed' this, they had to have that. They couldn't live without it – so they bought it. On credit, with credit, installment plans – you name it or however you name it, they asked for it.

Have you noticed: every commercial you see always says something similar to this "Only $8.99 a month".

It makes me laugh to hear how commercials avoid the obvious and they try to sell you on how something they say you just have to have only cost "X" amount of dollars a month. And to sweeten the deal they tell you it's only thirty five cents a day! Now that is a deal. What they fail to mention to you is how much it will cost you in the long run. They especially fail to mention most of the hidden fees, cost and taxes that are added to that wonderful low monthly rate.

But for arguments sake let's ignore that. Let's just go with the idea that it's only $8.99 a month.

We're going to say there is a fake internet company that lets you see any movie you want whenever you want and all you have to do to get this great wonderful service is – pay them $8.99 a month.

So if we do the math:

$8.99 x 1 year = $107.88 (12 months)
$8.99 x 2 years = $215.76
$8.99 x 3 years = $323.64
$8.99 x 4 years = $431.52
$8.99 x 5 years = $539.40
$8.99 x 10 years = $1,078.80
$8.99 x 43 years = $4,638.84

Wow, that sure adds up doesn't it?

Now you might be thinking that this is still not a lot of money to worry about for getting that wonderful service. But you fail to realize this one simple fact, that you need an internet provider to use this service – that my friend is another $29.99 a month, depending on your local provider.

One year of internet service totals: $359.88.
Two years of internet service totals: $719.76.
Five years of internet service totals: $1,799.40.

After 43 years of internet service the grand total you have paid out is: $15,474.84.

So to get that wonderful online 'watch movies' whenever you want service you need to pay the $8.99 a month plus the $29.99 (or more depending on your provider) for the internet service you need in order to watch these wonderful movies. Can you see how things quietly and secretly start adding up against you?

Now can you imagine having to do the same with everything else in life: the rent or mortgage, car payment, car insurance, taxes, electricity, cell phone, cable, on and on the list goes. Looking at it in this way gives you a long term view of what exactly is happening with you and your money.

MadMadMax
(a commenter wrote on one of my blogs)
   10 reasons why I have less money than yesterday;
   1. Federal taxes have increased
   2. State taxes have increased
   3.Local taxes have increased
   4.Auto insurance premiums have increased

5.Health insurance premiums have increased

6. Electricity rates have increased

7.Telephone rates have increased

8.The cost of all necessities has increased

9.My Boss is in the same boat, so they are spending less and no raises

10. I am spending yesterday's money today to survive till tomorrow.

Why YOU need to take Advantage

I point all this out not to overwhelm you, but to point out a simple over looked fact: you are the only one that can control your spending habits. There is no one else that is going to look out for you, to warn you about the pit falls that are out there. In order to get professional financial help, you have to pay for it – and even then, in the end the professional you are paying good hard earned money to help you with your finances, they will tell you that you are ultimately the one in control. They can only advise you on what to do, you have to make the decision and act upon it.

You may be worth $1.2 million dollars over a life time; you may be even worth more a lot more. I simply cannot predict your future. You may go to college and become an engineer who earns $30k a year or one who earns $60K a year – I simply do not know? What I do know is that you are the one, the only one, who can control what happens to the money you work so hard to earn.

So before you think of how cool the next new service or 'Hot' must have product might be and that it will only cost you $8.99 a month – why not factor in how much it will cost you over a year, five years, 10 years or over 43 years and then think about saving that money, investing it for your future?

If you live the average life span of 70 to 85 years – you will have spent more than 50% of your life working, depending on when and if you can afford to retire. In all those years of working you would have earned an estimated $1,200,000 dollars (or more). So you decide: do you let yourself be taken advantage of by those who want more money (your money) or do you save it, invest it and manage your money wisely. Why not take advantage of your savings and your investments to do what you want; say like – retire early, fulfill a dream or travel the world?

So I've proven to you that you are worth millions.

I have also warned you about those who are diligently seeking of ways to separate you from your millions (money).

My question to you is: What are you going to do about it?

A real decision is measured by the fact that you've taken a new action. If there's no action, you haven't truly decided.
~Tony Robbins

YOU ARE WORTH MILLIONS
HAVE A PLAN?

Do you have a plan?

I have just proven to you that you are worth millions – what are you going to do now? And no, it may sound funny but please don't joke about "I'm going to Disneyland". Honestly, have you thought about the future, what you want to do in life? Most young people have dreams; they make plans for the future, about what they want to be when they grow up.

What about your finances, your money, about your millions?

You may think I am stretching the issue here but think about it. What are your plans to keep most of the money you will work very hard to earn over your lifetime?

"He who fails to plan, plans to fail"
~ Proverb - unknown author

There is an old saying "time flies when you're having fun" and believe you me, time flies by when you're busy living and working. It is a subtle thing, you do not realize what is happening, but like everyone else in the world – one day you will look back on your life and wonder where did all the 'time' go?

Your plan for the future and as I am sure you have one, should include saving money and investing money. Be it for retirement, to fulfill a lifelong dream – whatever it may be. Saving and investing should be included into your plans for the future.

I know it's a shock to most people, the idea that you should 'SAVE' money! I also understand that most people say they save, they think they are saving money and in truth – they end up with very little saved at all.

I can say this because it has been reported that: nearly half of all Americans die owning less than $10,000 in financial assets.

Most people just don't think about saving or about investing and managing their money until it is usually too late.

A failure to plan

I have a family member that retired with $30,000 dollars to his name. He worked at a company that paid him about $90,000 dollars a year and he worked 30 long years before he was able to retire with a $30,000 annual pension. He is a wonderful person, a good hearted and very giving person. In fact, I believe him to be one of the best people I know. He just never planed ahead when it came to retirement. Even though he was getting closer to retirement He couldn't give up the habit of buying a brand new car every 2 yrs. He was too generous when helping people, family and friends.

If you look at his life as in what he has 'earned' over the last 30 years you will find that he earned millions. To be exact, he earned $2,700,000. That is not counting the money he earned before that particular employer and the money he is currently receiving from his pension during his retirement. Imagine earning $2.7 million dollars over the course of thirty years and when he retired all he had to his name was $30,000 dollars in cash.

Sadly enough he is spending the years he had 'planned' to have relaxing and enjoying with his family, working 40 hours a week in order to pay the bills. He does this because his debts and living expenses have completely outweighed the income he receives from his pension.

He didn't plan to retire this way, it just happened turn out this way. This was not a person who managed his money poorly, he has great credit – banks were fighting over his business whenever he walked in to get a loan. He was proud of the fact that he paid his bills on time and he never failed to pay anyone he owed money to. He merely failed to properly plan for his retirement and the money he did save for retirement – he always found a 'good' reason why to dip into his 401k plan or into his savings account.

He earned $2.7 million dollars during the span of thirty years and how much does he have left, zero. He used the last of his remaining money, the $30,000 as down payment to purchase himself a home in Florida.

It happened to him. It happens to thousands of millions of people and it can happen to you. Before you know it, time passes by and you are wondering to yourself: What happened? Why did this happen?

Finding the Money is not hard

People think that the hardest part about saving money is in finding the money to save. That's not true. In fact, finding the money is easy, being dedicated to saving money is what people truly find difficult to do. Most people know they need to save; this is why many people make it one of their top ten 'New Years' resolutions. This year, this year I am going to save more money. Then the next year comes along and there they are again making the same resolution they made last year.

As I mentioned before, you will need to work in order to live – so unless you are unemployed, making money is not the problem. The problem with saving comes from how you spend the money you earn.

Before we go any further let me say this.

Every person is unique; every life has its different challenges, obstacles and hardships to face. But your choices, your decisions taken over the course of your life has a large part in how you live your life and even in how and if you overcome those obstacles.

If you are young I want you to think about how every choice you make will affect every aspect of your life. Believe it or not, your choices, your decisions – you are in control. If you choose wrong because of an "I know" what I am doing attitude. Because you refuse to accept sound advice. You and only you alone are to blame for making your life that much more difficult for you to succeed in.

If you are older, if you have already made poor choices and are struggling with the burdens "you" put upon yourself. To you I say, suck it up, all is not lost. It will be harder, more difficult, you will have to sacrifice more – but you can change your life. You can make it better.

To you, the few who through no fault of your own

have been put in situations that make life - make reaching success more difficult. To you I say do not be dismayed. Do not surrender or give up. You can make it. You did not put yourself here, but this does not have to define you. You can do better.

That is the beauty of time.

As long as you have time, you can do what is necessary to change tomorrow.

When it comes to time, time is what helps you and I convert small amounts of money – into a large sum of money. Time is what can be used to change a life, convert dreams to reality, to create value from what others consider worthless. This is why I want to drill into your head, you are worth millions, yes millions over time – do not squander it.

Let us stop here to do some math.

Let's stop for a minute and let's do some math. To some this may be common knowledge, but for the purposes of helping me make my point – indulge me.

Let's look at Money and what can be accomplished when saved over time.

Starting balance: $0.00 dollars.

Deposit $500.00 dollars a month for 516 months (516 months = 43 years)

@ a compounded interest of a low estimated average of 1% (* just a study, ignore any balance requirements) The total amount saved would be: $322,189.31

* I used a financial calculator at: www.timevalue.com

So basically you would have saved using 2012 low saving accounts interest rates, a whopping total of $322,189.31.

Now you may be thinking something down the line of: where on God's green earth am I going to find $500 dollars to save every month? And true, it may be difficult for you now, but let me interject something here. I know people who have purchased new cars every two years for the last thirty years. Oh and by the way - they only drive their car on Sunday. I know people who own boats that they have been paying on for the last twenty years and that doesn't count the cost associated with title, insurance and let's not forget the wonderful dock fees. Yet with all these cost they only use the boat possibly 2 to 4 times a month?

It's a given, people are always saying they don't have money to save or can't find the money they need to save because they do not want to face the reality of their spending habits. It is not until they are under a severe financial crisis that they realize that they are going to have to let go of some of the luxuries they have surrounded themselves with.

So the question should be — how?
How do I save?
What do I have to do?

Planning for the future

Whether you're planning for retirement (which young people often fail to do at an early age) or planning just for tomorrow, you should incorporate these tips into any plan you create.

(**Side note**) Remember, I do not know your individual circumstance or your plans for the future. You may be planning for retirement, planning to retire at age thirty or you may be older just starting to think about retirement. Or you may be planning to be rich and successful at age 25. I simply do not know. These tips I present here are basic, generalized and can be molded into whatever your goals and plans are.

(*****) This was written to an intended audience of teenagers and young adults who are just starting out in life. Meaning they have no debt, no children, possibly no work (job). But it can be applied to any situation with sleight modifications and of course - a little more sacrifice and struggle.

When it comes to planning for the future - time is our very best friend or it can be our worst enemy. While most people want everything "now" and find it extremely challenging to patiently wait, the successful person uses time to his/her advantage.

Most financial advisors speak of retirement and they all mention one key factor 'Time'. When we hear the word time we tend to think: retirement as in many years from now, old and why plan for when I am almost dead. We struggle with the concept of time because we believe we should have "things now".

But as I stated before, no matter what side of the tracks you come from - rich or poor, you will probably work most of your life away. All you have is time and how you manage that time and the resources you have accumulated over that time is what truly counts.

So the question remains, what do we factor in as part of our plan, when creating a 'financial plan' for the future?

No. 1: Start by controlling your debt.

Pay off expensive debts, and then accelerate savings in earnest.

Many are concerned about how college students are graduating from college and are saddled with debt before they even enter the work force. While this is true - I would suggest that young adults are entering college with debt and they continue to create more debt as they go along. Yes this debt is often carried by parents; but the habit of poorly managing money will stay with them long after Mom and Dad are no longer carrying the bag (paying for child's expenses).

Learning how to successfully manage money is a whole topic unto itself. There is a reason why hundreds of books have been written on the subject - there is simply too much to cover. So I will make it simple and hope that you encourage yourself to seek out more knowledge on the subject.

When I say control your debt, I do not simply refer to credit cards. As mentioned before, debt is everything that puts a constant drain on your money. Companies are hard at work trying to get you to buy a product or a service from them. They sell it to you as a small nominal fee - it's only $8.99 a month. All these services, credit cards, you name it are sapping your wealth and are being used to drain your finances, that is to move your millions into their pockets.

Analyze your spending

Using a free online tool such as Mint.com, check where your money is going and where you might be able to cut back to add more to your savings. Many banks offer free money tracking tools through online accounts, along with automated reminders about savings.

No. 2: Start Saving "NOW"!

Why did I put control your debt as no.1 and saving as your no.2 step?

The truth is most people, especially out of control spenders like young adults, believe they can't save because they have no money to save. What most people do not realize is that they are basically waiting for the end of the month to save money after they have purchased, spent and then paid all of their monthly debts. By doing it this way you will never have money at the end of the month to save because you spent it all before you could even begin to save.

In order to save money you need to make it (that is earn it), then you need to manage it (control - plan on how to use it and spend it). The first step of any plan used in managing money should be to 'save money'. Many financial advisors call it "paying yourself first". You will find that if you save first, as in pay yourself first, you will always have money to save. Yes, you will have to sacrifice something else in return, but instead of sacrificing your future, why not sacrifice something you can live without?

(*) I cannot with good conscious tell you how much money to save, that is up to you. Many financial advisors say you should start with a minimum of 10 % of your income. I am not going to pretend that I am familiar with your personal individual financial circumstance, so I leave 'how much to save' up to you.

The important thing is that you SAVE.

The time value of money

Saving a small amount each day can do wonders for your portfolio in the long term. For example, "Not spending $1.50 a day on a soda can have a big impact on a person's financial future," says David Bruzzese, coauthor of The Teen's Guide to Personal Finance. This concept is particularly valuable for younger people, who can accumulate a lot of money over the years by taking simple steps to cut wasteful daily expenses.

No. 3: Start and stick to a budget

Budgets are not the most exciting topic when it comes to finance, but your budget will underlie all of your wealth-building efforts and keep you on track with everyday expenses and savings. Just identifying your regular expenses and bills can help you pin down where your money is going. There may also be some fat that could be cut, which could translate to more savings.

In your budget you should have 3 important elements:

a. Saving

You should be saving money for three particular things. This should be saving money for the future (retirement), saving money for investing (when I say investing it can be in stocks, bonds or starting a business - you decide) and then you should also save for emergencies, after all things do happen, the car breaks down, you lose your job, an emergency fund is used to protect savings and investments from being used in any emergency that arises.

b. Tracking

A budget should do several things for you: track your current expenses so you know what, where and why? You should have a clear understanding of how you are using and spending your money. You should also use it to figure out where the 'fat' is in order to cut unnecessary expenses that occur and so that it can be put to better use.

Last but not least, it should help you stay on track. Having a physical track record helps you to easily see your progress and keeping a record also forces you to have a written accountable record on how you are managing your finances (there should be no guessing).

c. Allow for changes

While it may be foolish to keep making changes to a budget - what I am trying to say is: nothing is set in stone. Things happen, life happens; you have to be able to make corrections, changes, alterations to your budget and to your plan.

Do not make your budget too rigid. You need to build in flexibility, or your plan will break under pressure. Give yourself some breathing room to make mistakes, for a treat and to make adjustments as the situations in your life change. For instance, what if your car insurance rate goes up, gas prices climb or your rent rises?

The perfect plan would be to save for all three saving agenda's: savings, investing and emergency fund. But your income may dictate that this will not be feasible. So put a time frame and a plan in motion to slowly work up to having all three but start saving. As things improve make necessary changes to improve on your plan.

All I am saying is: do your best to work your plan, just be aware that it may need some tweaks along the way.

No. 4: Take an appropriate amount of risk.

Sometimes playing it safe can be more dangerous than taking some risk. My advice to the young people of today people is - learn how to take 'calculated risk'.

What is Risk?

Risk: is an exposure to the chance of injury or loss; a hazard or dangerous chance.

Rich people are successful people because they know when to take risk. After all risk is a part of life; everything we do has a degree of risk in it. If you take a test there is a chance you will fail. If you take a bath, there is a risk, a chance you will fall and get hurt. Life has its risky moments. You simply need to learn how to properly manage risk.

If life is full of risk, then one of the important keys to life is in knowing when to take a risk.

That key, knowing when to take a risk – that is called "Calculated Risk".

Just like in life, nothing is exactly the same and in this case there is "Risk" and then there is "Calculated Risk".

What is Calculated Risk?

Calculated Risk: is a possible chance of failure, the probability of which is estimated (meaning you count the cost) before some action is undertaken.

Knowing the difference between these two risks is very important if you want to succeed in life. The reason is because one risk is actually more 'riskier' than the other.

The many forms of Investing

It's your life and you should know yourself better than anyone else. All I am suggesting is that your success will not solely rely on you saving money. You have to live, so you will be required to spend money. You may get married, have kids, you may even get ill or have a tragedy occur in your family. It makes no difference how much money you have saved up, one illness, a prolonged stay at a hospital fighting a health issue can deplete most or all of your savings very quickly.

My advice is to save, invest and if at all possible create several forms of income streams. You do this by starting a business or purchasing an established successful business'. And we all know that this requires a certain amount of risk.

(* We will talk more about investing and creating more than one stream of income in a later chapter)

"America is an idea, but it's an idea that brings with it some baggage, like power brings responsibility. It's an idea that brings with it equality, but equality even though it's the highest calling, is the hardest to reach. The idea that anything is possible, that's one of the reasons why I'm a fan of America. It's like hey, look there's the moon up there, let's take a walk on it, bring back a piece of it. That's the kind of America that I'm a fan of."
~Bono

You are Worth Millions
Think about money logically

Most people when they think about money fall into one of two categories: The first is emotional which usually leads to irrational thinking. The second is logical which tends to cause other people to think you are cold, callus, heartless, uncaring and most popular of all selfish and greedy.

Being logical is simply another way of saying smart or being wise.

While I would never suggest you remove your emotions from the equation – on how you think about money. I would recommend that you think clearly and logically when it comes to the issue of money. People believe that it has to be one or the other: you give because you are good, you care or you are selfish, heartless and greedy because you don't give.

What people fail to see is that there is a large grey area; it's not all black and white, right or wrong.

Let me put it to you this way. If all you had saved in the bank was $600 and you needed that money to pay the rent that was due next week. If a close friend or a family member came to you, said that they were in great financial need and they wanted to know if you could lend them some money. That they would not ask if it wasn't because, they really needed your help.

Would you give them your rent money?

Would you put yourself, your spouse, and your children at risk of being kicked out of your home and lend that person the money?

What if you knew this person, they were close, they were very good people – would that make a difference in your decision to lend them the money?

Some people would 'No'.

They would logically think about the situation and come to the conclusion that despite their great desire to help this person, they themselves cannot afford to risk the well being of their family to help this individual. This in turn would probably cause the person in need to think that you were selfish, greedy, uncaring because they know you have the money to help but will not.

Some would say 'Yes'.

They would feel the need to help and they would put their family at risk hoping nothing goes wrong. Because after all the right thing to do when someone is in need, is to help?

But things usually have a way of not going well. These kind caring people fail to pay the rent because they lent the money they did have, the individual they lent the money to is in need and unable to help them in return by paying back the borrowed money. Now the family is behind on the rent, they can't seem to catch up and things spiral even further as they face being evicted from their home.

Now all this sounds like a bit of an exaggeration, but this can happen and has happened.

This is why it is important to be logical when you think about money. You may say that it is more important to help someone in need because you can't see how helping someone in need is not as important as saving money for a rainy day in the future. The thing is that the money you are saving is not money that is just being horded. The money you are putting aside should have a purpose. This money could important, like as in money used for your dream, education, to care for a medical expense in the future or some other important need.

I heard a friend say that "people are saving money for a rainy day while their (grown) children are financially struggling. They do not realize that for that child it is raining – why not help them?"

This is not wrong; I would never suggest against helping someone who is in true need, especially your own child. But we should also remember that you are saving money, investing your money – the money you worked hard to earn, with a purpose, a reason. The money you are saving and investing is there to protect you, to provide the things you need when you are no longer able to work.

It is said that the average person will live (life expectancy) an estimated fifteen to twenty years after they retire. This is a long time to live with just the money you have put aside. You may be thinking that you will have social security to live on, but considering that it has been reported that if social security is not overhauled it will go bankrupt by the year 2033 – I certainly wouldn't count on it.

You factor in that in the end, you will never reach your dreams, goals, build a business or send your children to college, much less retire comfortably if you keep giving all your savings away to help others – even if it is to help someone in true need. It sounds wonderful, but life, real life is nothing like the movies.

Kimberly Palmer wrote this in her "50 Ways to Improve Your Finances in 2013" article for U.S. News, Money section.

31: Protect your money from your children.

Baby boomers have been generous toward their adult children, inviting them to move back home and offering them direct financial support. But often, that kind of generosity hurts parents' own retirement nest egg. In fact, even the parents of two Olympic gold medalists, Gabby Douglas and Ryan Lochte, revealed major financial troubles of their own. Before putting their own financial security at risk, parents should consider whether they can really afford the help they're offering.

Kimberly Palmer is a senior editor for U.S. News
Money article: 50 Ways to Improve Your Finances in 2013

How many people, seniors, some who even provide full time care for their grandchildren are suffering, barely living, simply surviving day to day because they didn't save for the future, for retirement, for their golden years.

Please, do not be offended but: I ask you, who will help you?

Do we live in a utopian world where everyone takes care of their fellow man and no one suffers unnecessary needs? Or when you walk the streets, spend time at the mall; do you notice the poverty, the overwhelming need that is out there?

Again, I am not talking about greed, selfishness, and the hording of wealth. What I am talking about is responsibility, being prudent and wise. Learning how to be like the wise ant in the old fable – working diligently and storing up for the winter when he is no longer able to work.

You have to think logically.

Just another Trap

The world is fill with financial pitfalls and traps. One of the most deceptive financial traps around is so aptly called "the rat race".

Doctor or lawyer, high paid employee or business owner – anyone can be trapped in the "rat race". The term rat race basically means that no matter how much money you make, you never have enough. Not out of greed, but because you never have enough money to sustain your lifestyle.

Imagine if you will a Doctor sitting at his lavish expensive beach front home. He walks over to his boat that is sitting in the dock at his private slip and he is wondering if he should spend the day sailing or maybe he should take a nice relaxing drive in his expensive $100,000 dollar vehicle. He has expensive clothing on, a diamond encrusted watch and all the luxuries you could ever dream of. You wouldn't hesitate to think that he had it all.

But in truth, what you might consider success is truly the ill fated trappings of that devilish game called the rat race.

While it all looks wonderful from the outside, the truth is this doctor doesn't have time to spend on his boat or to casually drive around town in his new expensive car. He has to get to the office, meet patients, and find new clients because he has all these luxuries that are eating him out of house and home.

He can't afford to stop working, he has to find more and more work because even though he has all these wonderful toys – he is cash poor. Every penny he makes goes into maintaining that lavish lifestyle you and I so desperately covet for ourselves. It's not only the poor who have too much month and not enough money – millions of middle class people and some you may even consider to be rich, have the same financial problem poor people have. The bills are simply way too much.

They have allowed irrational thought to cloud their judgment when it came to finances, to money. I am a Doctor so I am expected to have the big house, fancy car – even if I weren't a doctor appearance is what matters and I have to keep up with the Jones' next door. The sad thing is you don't have to be middle class or rich to have this type of irrational thinking.

Poor people are just as guilty as the middle class and the rich. Spending money they don't have for the sake of appearance, because everyone has a laptop, an Iphone or name brand apparel so of course "I have to have that too". After all if you want to be in, if you want to be part of the click, the group – you have to have it even if you can't afford it.

With this irrational financial mind set we struggle to make it month to month, paycheck to paycheck, as we wonder who is at fault? Who can I blame for my financial situation?

Money is a tool

Do not be fooled, money is simply a tool to be used. A tool that can be used like a precision instrument such as a scalpel in the hands of a skilled surgeon can save a life. Yet that same tool, that same scalpel can be poorly handled by a layman with no surgical knowledge – which would be a recipe for disaster.

Like a tool, money should be managed wisely and to do so you need a 'Plan'. A plan clearly spells out where you are headed and what it is you intend to achieve. After the plan is formulated you need to create a budget, which controls spending, builds savings and helps to acquire investments. As I stated before, your budget should factor in three things: saving for future goals, saving for unforeseen emergencies (emergency fund), and savings that are used for investing (stocks, bonds, business).

I understand that I am speaking in ideal terms; that you may first have to save up and build an emergency fund to draw from in case of an emergency before you can even think of investing. But the point is that you should work towards never using the money that is set aside for savings and for investing. If money is a tool it has to be managed properly in order to have success.

How to better understand the principal of money as a tool?

Money provides time: Money is a tool that can be used to provide you with more time to do what you need done – as in priority. For example, you are a writer and you make money by writing books (that's a given). So how can money be used as a tool to help you prioritize what needs to be done? Simple, instead of you mowing your lawn, you pay someone else to mow it for you. This in return gives you the free time needed to finish the book you are writing. The same goes for everything else, washing your car, doing the laundry; it sounds odd but the more free time you create from "paying" someone else to do your time consuming work, the more time you have to do what is most important to you.

Money helps you meet your goals: So let's stay with the writer theme. You have finished your book and now it's time to promote it, after all, who will buy it if no one knows it exists. So now you use money to buy advertising that promotes your book even while you sleep. You go on book tours, traveling around town, the city and even throughout the entire United States - that requires money. So money is the tool that facilitates the promotion of your book that you have written while that same money is also paying to have your other obligations such as having your lawn maintenance meet.

Money makes life easier: Continuing with the writer theme you have to wonder, what are the benefits to all this work? The answer is simple: money. Assuming you have written a great book, your promotions are working well and the book tour was a success - the outcome should be that you are selling hundreds of thousands of books. So the tool you used (money) to help you create has also helped you meet your goals and now it begins to give back to you a reward; that reward is money. Now this is also considered an investment. Why is it an investment? Because after your book is selling you can go home and write another book while your book continues to sell - it's what's called in the business world as residual income. Basically it's a system or process that you set in place that continues to give you a return on your investment (money).

Of course the above is an overly simplified example, but I am simply using it as a means to illustrate how money can be used as a tool to further ones goals in life. If you do not believe me just ask JK Rowling, the creator of the Harry Potter book series, which has made her the richest writer ever. Did you know it took her 5 years to write her first book?

Today, the name JK Rowling is widely known in many parts of the world for creating the Harry Potter series, but it wasn't so about a decade ago. In fact, in 1993 she was on welfare (public assistance) and tending to a baby while she wrote her first novel,

Harry Potter and the Philosopher's Stone. And while her story may be a "rags to riches" success story, the principal is still the same.

How you think about money, how you manage money – logical or irrational, money is simply a tool. A tool that can be used to create success, create wealth and opportunities. Or a tool that can be mismanaged, it can be wasted and it can even become a destructive force in your life.

Like tools, money should be used to build, to create not simply to sustain. It is easy to be pulled into the trap that so many have fallen into; the belief that money is something you simply spend in a means to get by, to move along the many days of life with no purpose, no goal and no dream. Living one day at a time, unaware as time slips by.

It's your money, how much of it do plan on keeping?

Do you plan on retiring or working for the rest of your natural life, until the day you breathe your last breath?

Money is a tool, to be used in any which way you so desire. It can be used for good, it can also be used for bad – but only you decide.

You are Worth Millions
Acquire knowledge

Learning is a lifelong goal.

Learning is the lifelong process of transforming information and experience into knowledge, skills, behaviors, and attitudes.

I might add: It is not dependent solely upon classes and courses – though these can be very useful tools for learning

It does not always require a degree, certificate, or grade to prove its worth – though clearly these have social value that most people would be unwise to ignore

It does require in varying degrees, and in varying

times and circumstances – activities like practice, reflection, interaction with the environment (in the broadest sense), and social interaction. The latter, in particular, can be greatly facilitated by the range of new technologies for communication and collaboration now available to us.

It does not always happen consciously though I think that those who strive for a more conscious approach to learning throughout their lives tend to be more successful in pretty much whatever way they define success.

As defined by Webster, education is the process of educating or teaching, and 'educate' is "to develop the knowledge, skill, or character," the broader perspective of this definition is to transmit the knowledge onto the next generation so that the individuals can build their lives on the principles learned.

Education, as is normally understood, is not only what is taught to the students in schools, colleges and universities rather it is a lifelong process. When we say a lifelong process, we are encompassing all the learning experiences a human has during his life. This process never ends and keeps on adding to an individual's personality. When we talk about teaching at school, it turns out in a person's life in the form of the implementation of that education in a person's professional life. When we talk about education from a church, a priest or any religious scholar, we mean the effects of that education or learning on the person's soul. Moreover another form is what we learn from our own experiences and observations. Thus we can't just restrict education to secular or in what is being taught to a person; rather education can come from observation or a person's own experience as well. Thus teaching or educating is not always a necessary part of learning; one can learn new things on their own as well.

Once in a parent-teacher meeting, a teacher asked the parents how do they judge that their kids are learning something new daily from the school, the most common answer was that kids do their home work regularly which shows that the child is learning new things. The teacher replied to the parents that just because he is doing his homework regularly does not mean that he is also learning, rather you should cross-check that what he is learning by encouraging him to take part in general discussions and ask his opinion about various life issues. Involving him in the decision-making process and giving him the opportunity to provide solutions to different issues will open up his mind and broaden his horizons. The learning achieved by implementation can never be replaced by theory. Practical is more important than just theory.

A beautiful quote by Bill Beattie about education is worth mentioning here, the author said "The aim of education should be to teach us rather how to think, than what to think – rather to improve our minds, so as to enable us to think for ourselves, than to load the memory with the thoughts of other men." This is the true purpose of education where one can expect education to broaden a person's horizon and leave him to ask questions in order to learn new things. There is no better way to learn than to ask questions.

Here is a question some might ask: How do you think it is possible to keep learning and to continue to learn with the very limited time there is. Especially for people that are working and or have children?

My answer would be: find the time and take note of the things that happen around you.

Yes I know it's a simple answer. So let me go into greater detail.

You would be amazed at how much free time people have. As reported in the American Time Use Survey Summary release Friday, June 22, 2012, people on an average day spend 5.8 to 5.2 hours occupied in leisure activities such as watching T.V, sports and socializing. The report also stated that watching TV was the leisure activity that occupied the most time, an estimate 2.8 hours per day.

The American Time Use Survey Summary

-- On an average day, nearly everyone age 15 and over engaged in some sort of leisure activity (95 percent), such as watching TV, socializing, or exercising. Of those who engaged in leisure activities, men spent more time in these activities (5.8 hours) than did women (5.2 hours).

-- Watching TV was the leisure activity that

occupied the most time (2.8 hours per day), accounting for about half of leisure time, on average, for those age 15 and over. Socializing, such as visiting with friends or attending or hosting social events, was the next most common leisure activity, accounting for nearly three-quarters of an hour per day.

http://www.bls.gov/news.release/atus.nr0.htm

Now I am sure that this report was done with the upmost accuracy, but I would like to suggest that people spend even more time doing leisurely activities - take for instance Facebook. All those minutes reading your news feed in bed, messaging friends over lunch, and browsing photos on the bus really add up. It has been reported that time spent on Facebook's mobile site and apps per month (441 minutes) has finally surpassed usage of its classic website (391 minutes) — for Americans who use both Facebook interfaces according to the latest report from comScore.

We have the time, to learn something new every day - but for most people, that time is usually spent doing something leisurely. Don't get me wrong, you need time to de-stress, relax, wind down and be entertained. I am not talking against spending time socializing with family, friends and neighbors. What I am referring to is the understanding that in order to succeed you need to learn, to self educate, increase your knowledge base and the understanding of the world around you - and that takes time.

Like money, time is also something you have to learn how to manage. You have to condition yourself and create a desire within yourself to want to learn. You should be curious about things, how they work - ask questions if you don't understand something. You should seek to learn something that will be beneficial to you.

Learning is a process and while some may be content with just being, many have found success through the simple act of trying to improve upon a situation or an idea. Take for instance Mr. Moshe Weiss. Mr. Wiess is a Rabbi who found himself on the popular TV show Shark Tank. Shark tank is basically an ABC reality TV show. On the show, participants pitch their business ideas and investment opportunities to a 5 team member board of millionaire / billionaire entrepreneurs and business executives, in hopes that one or several of these entrepreneurs will love the idea and invest their money and expertise.

When he was asked how he came up with the idea he said this "Because I love my iPad®.... A good friend of mine gave me an iPad2® as a gift. Immediately I wasn't happy with the sound and tried to use my hand in order to amplify it. After one day my hand was getting tired so I cut out a band-aid box and affixed it to the speaker area to replace my cupped hand. It worked and the SoundBender® was born!"

On Mr. Wiess website: www.thesoundbender.com, he goes on to explain "That very week I began making clay and wax molds trying it out on my iPad® and started developing the prototype with a local manufacturer and industrial designer. Soon after what began as a wax mold and toothpicks was transformed into 3D CAD models for prototyping and injection molding. After perfecting and re-perfecting the SoundBender for improved functionality and sleek design I am truly proud of the result... "

Mr. Wiess is a Rabbi, he knew nothing of business, of 3D CAD, or injection molding – but I am sure that when Mr. Weiss found himself with this dilemma (the lack of knowledge), he sought out a solution, had an idea, started to do research and to learn all that he could; the result was that he created something new. He now has a business, a high profile investor backing him and even a bit of celebrity status - all because he took the time to question, inquire and to learn.

Side note: You may be asking yourself "where did the Rabbi get the money to do all this prototyping and injection molding?" Well, SoundBender raised over $8000 dollars in funding via the online crowd-sourcing platform Kickstarter, exceeding its fundraising goal of $4500. But we will talk more about that in a later chapter.

Acquiring specific knowledge on money

There is a saying: Knowledge is power. While this may be a well known and used verse, it is often misunderstood.

The act of accumulating knowledge is not power. Unless you plan on entering a TV trivia quiz game show, an over abundance of information is basically useless. Information is just that, a collection of facts, figures, equations and formulas. Having data, an accumulation of information does nothing if it is not informative, by this I mean that if it has no purpose, no intended goal it does nothing for you.

It is important to acquire specific knowledge, knowledge that is directed toward a single purpose, a single goal – money. I am not saying that you shouldn't smell the flowers as you enjoy life, or that you shouldn't learn how to ride a bike, drive a car or fly a plane. What I am saying is that you should take time to learn the facts about money, how it works, how to save it, invest it and so forth. It goes without saying, that any information you learn should be acquired with the intent of putting said knowledge into practice.

Jen Smith is a perfect example of how a person can accumulate knowledge, specific knowledge to attain a specific goal. As she describes it, one night, while working the graveyard shift at a donut shop and pouring coffee for a homeless woman, she realized that she was only one paycheck away from being homeless herself.

She calls this her "wake-up call" which motivated her by fear of an uncertain future; she opened the Yellow Pages, called professional dog trainers and negotiated an unpaid apprenticeship. Less than a year later, she was hired by her mentor. A couple years later, she started her own successful dog-training school.

Over the course of the next couple of years, she made it her mission to learn everything she could about personal finance, investing, entrepreneurship and lifestyle design. As she acquired this knowledge, she created a plan that would allow her and her husband to be free of their money worries.

By the age of 40, she was 100% debt free and had over a million dollars in the bank!

Today, she professes to spend each new day doing whatever she and her family chooses.

She promotes the "closet millionaire" life style. According to her you wouldn't have any clue that they were millionaires. "Our family lives a typical middle-class lifestyle with one fantastic exception– we only work when we want to. Financial freedom affords us the gift of free time."

I believe that knowledge is not power. Power comes from the ability to acquire knowledge that is applicable to the need in which you want to overcome and succeed in.

"Knowledge will forever govern ignorance; and a people who mean to be their own governors must arm themselves with the power which knowledge gives."
~ James Madison

You are Worth Millions
Don't be greedy?

You may be one of the few who will confuse what I am teaching, advocating and exhorting —as GREED.

I am not telling you to be stingy, greedy, to be a miser or a shyster. I am not asking you to find ways to cheat people out of their hard earned money. I am also not asking you to deprive yourself of simple pleasure in order to save .15 cents. What I want is for you to avoid being manipulated and cheated by those who want to quietly separate you out of your hard earned money. I do not wish you to be greedy but rather that you have the financial freedom necessary so that you may be able to do worth wide things such as give to those who are in need.

I know that some will think this odd; this book

actually promotes that child like saying: "Don't be greedy, give to the needy".

I say this because the truth is if you have nothing, how can you give something?

I know, you're thinking to yourself that you do not need money, that money is not the only way to help people who are in need. That you can give of your time, your talents, your knowledge and experience. That you can give out of a caring loving heart. And that is true.

But let me offer these words of wisdom imparted to me by my father-in-law just before I married his daughter:

"Love cannot pay the rent...."

What my soon to be in-law was telling me was that yes he knew I loved his daughter, but no amount of love, caring, emotions can put bread on the table or pay the rent when it is due. Love can cause you to work and the hard work you accomplish will create an income which will pay for food, clothing, rent and amenities that will keep your marriage happy.

It is said: Financial problems only account for 5 percent of divorces. But, 70 percent of married couples report some kind of money problems.

According to a 2009 study by Jeffrey Dew at the Utah State University, one of the best indicators of marital discord is what he terms "financial disagreements." Couples who "disagree about finances once a week" are over 30 percent more likely to get divorced than couples that report "disagreeing about finances a few times a month." Disagreeing about finance basically means fighting about money.

According to Dew, couples who disagree about money less than once per month run a 30 to 40 percent increase in the risk of divorce. This rate increases steeply when the partners fight several times per month, once a week, several times a week, to almost daily, when the risk increases to 125 percent to 160 percent.

In his study, Dew examined the responses of 2,800 couples surveyed in 1987 by the National Survey of Families and Households, who were contacted again in 1992, "and asked if they were still married." Of all the common items on the agenda of domestic disputes - chores, in-laws, spending time together, sex and money - "money disputes were the best harbinger of divorce."

Dew's metric of percent of increase in the risk of divorce may be a bit murky, but fights about money carry a big price. People may fight about how to spend what they have, but more often couples wake up too late to the cost of high living, which is debt. In extreme cases, debt becomes like an unwelcome stranger in their marriage, and recriminations and bickering soon take a toll.
www.divorcesource.com

We live in a world that is driven by money. As I stated before, there is always an exception to the rule. You may be just like Mr. Suelo you may decide to live outside the confines of today's society. You could go out into the desert and live in caves, eat off the land and that may be ok with you – but what about your wife, your children? Or when you are old and need medical attention? And most of all, how can you give, be able to help someone else, when you have so little – or in Mr. Suelo's case, you have nothing at all.

So like my father-in-law said: Love can't pay the rent. Neither can it help you feed the hungry, cloth the naked, or give shelter to the homeless. It sounds nice and again I am not promoting greed or hoarding, but in order to help, you need to have what is needed (money) in order to supply the need.

Another reason why saving and investing is so important?

Here's why: Retirement is expensive, and it can last a long time. Most people will have to save a substantial portion of their earnings over their working lifetimes if they want to retire comfortably. If they don't take the opportunities they're given to invest for retirement, they quickly fall behind, never to catch up.

Most Americans are failing to save enough for retirement:

- Half of Americans aren't contributing to a

retirement plan at all, according to a survey last year by LIMRA, a trade organization for financial services.

- Most of those who are saving haven't saved much; 60% of workers polled by the Employee Benefit Research Institute had less than $25,000.

- One researcher estimates that half of workers who are now middle class will be near or below the poverty line in retirement. Teresa Ghilarducci, a professor of economics at the New School for Social Research, said research from the school's Schwartz Center for Economic Policy Research shows that three-quarters of adults ages 50 to 64 have so little saved that the money won't provide a significant supplement to their Social Security checks.

Not about being GREEDY

It never changes, when you talk about money it is sure to happen, people start to call you greedy, selfish, that all you care about is money. Some people go to the extreme of believing that money is the root of all evil and therefore you are evil and corrupt.

I am not here to argue the philosophical. I believe that all men are created equal (men and women alike). We all have the potential to do evil, be evil and committee horrendous acts of cruelty. I hope and pray that good, the good that is also in the hearts of all men will ultimately prevail. My belief is that money, be it any form of currency or treasure that man covets – will bring forth what is already in the heart of that individual.

With that said, my goal is to help young people understand that they should think of the future. Be prepared, prepare and be ready for what lies before you. You will get old, you will not be able to work all the days of your life and if you have dreams for the future, you have to work at making them come true. It is not about greed.

"A man too busy to take care of his health is like a mechanic too busy to take care of his tools."
~Spanish proverb

Sometimes ideals often have a way of getting in the way of common sense.

A few months back (2012) I was sitting with a friend just talking about general things and the subject of money came up. The economy is bad, the recession has been slowly dragging along and it's not hard to have the subject of money simply casually come up.

He confided in me that times were very difficult for him. Financially speaking he wasn't poor or going hungry, he was just simply making due. He was way past the age of physically being able to work and it bothered him that he was unable to help people. He had always been a very caring and giving man, as a religious person he found it to be a personal obligation to help his fellow man whenever he possibly could. But now, basically living on the bare minimum he sees friends, family and others in need and he is unable to help – financially speaking. At times he says that he is unable to even give of his free time, such as volunteer work, because gas is so expensive and he cannot afford to make the extra trips into town.

I could see the sincerity of his words in his eyes, the pain he suffered in his heart could be heard in his voice. As we talked I couldn't help but stutter as my emotions weld up inside me. I thought I was going to cry right there and then. There was nothing I could do for him, this was a proud man, he didn't need a hand out — what he wanted was to be able to help. What he wanted was to have extra money so that he could be able to help others.

I am not promoting greed. I am not promoting a life of hoarding money, living as a stingy miser who will do anything to save a penny. That is not what I am writing about.

The average person will work an estimated 43 yrs of their life, in that time they will earn and estimated $1.2 million dollars, possibly even more. What I want is for you to manage that money wisely. To take advantage of the opportunities you have to make your dreams come true if possible. I want you to learn how to manage your money, to invest so that you can be in a position to help yourself and to help others whenever possible. That if your dream is to spend your golden years skiing or helping feed the homeless —that you will be able to do just that.

Money is not the solution, it is not the answer to all your problems, and it is not the source of your happiness. But money can make your life a bit easier, it can afford you the opportunity to help make someone else's life easier. In a time of crisis people call out for donations and how wonderful it is to be able to say – here I can give.

It's not about greed.

"What material success does is provide you with the ability to concentrate on other things that really matter. And that is being able to make a difference, not only in your own life, but in other people's lives."
~Oprah Winfrey

"To me, money is a means to do good. I reached a point in my life where I had enjoyed tremendous business success that afforded my family everything we could possibly want. My wife and I then decided that we could use our wealth to make a difference. So we created the Broad Foundations to do four things: to improve urban public education, to support innovative scientific and medical research, to foster art appreciation for audiences worldwide and to support civic initiatives in Los Angeles."
~Eli Broad

You are Worth Millions
How can I make more

By now you have to be thinking it: I am going to need more? How can I make more money?

There are plenty of justifiable reasons why you may need more money, not out of greed but of necessity. Your dream may be to retire early and spend all your free time giving back to the community through local volunteer work. Your dream may be to be the first in your family to get a college education and you want to be financially able to accomplish this dream and even help another member of your family to do the same. Your dream may be to start a business, to be financially stable enough to be able to give to others who are in need, such as feeding the hungry, helping the homeless or supporting charitable organizations. Whatever your dream or goals are you may need more money to accomplish them or to be able to do more with the free time the extra money affords you. Imagine if you were able to retire in 23 years instead of 43 years – the good you could do if you could afford to support yourself and still be able to help others?

Your dream may be as simple and as personal as simply being able to afford children. Growing up in a family of seven brothers and sister, struggling under the weight of poverty – I can understand Melissa Will when she says "I would like to have some realistic idea of when we can afford to have kids".

Personal finance is never really about the money. It's about what you can and can't do. To Melissa Will, personal finance is about starting a family – specifically, why she just can't have a baby now, or anytime soon.

From an outside look you would think that Melissa was living the American dream. She married her longtime boyfriend Ryan in 2011 and soon after they bought a lovely home. They are hard working responsible young people who have done their best to avoid getting into debt with credit cards and student loans. But when you take a deeper look the reality of their personal finance math is harsh: They earn about $3,000 each month, and they spend about $3,000 a month. They are homeowners, and they have avoided deep student loan and credit card debt that plagues many 20-somethings, putting them on solid footing. But they aren't getting ahead. If they moved forward with their family plans, they couldn't afford the $1,000 monthly health insurance bill that would come when Melissa tried to add family members to her employer's health care plan.

Melissa Will is featured in an article by Bob Sullivan, Columnist, NBC News
Article: Red Tape intervention: Can fighting fees help this young couple afford a baby?

Whatever the case may be – you may find that despite the estimated $1.2 million dollars the average person earns over a life span [est. 43 yrs of working] you may desire to earn more money to accomplish a better quality of life, goals, dreams and desires.

In a book I wrote for children: For children how to become Rich, Successful & do well in school, I brought up a very important fact about making money, which was – anyone can do it.

Not just making some money but making millions and even at a very early age, for example:

Fraser Doherty

When you think of making millions, you probably don't think about jam, Smuckers or Welches notwithstanding. But one Scottish youth, Fraser Doherty, made his millions off just that.

Doherty began making jam from fruit and fruit juice, based on his grandma's recipe, out of his parents' kitchen at the tender age of 15. He mostly sold to friends and fellow churchgoers, but demand quickly spiked, outstripping his ability to produce.

Since starting, Doherty's jam has spread to virtually every grocery chain in the UK and Ireland, including the biggest UK retailer of them all, Sainsbury. His product, SuperJam, comes in a wide array of unique flavors, including blueberry & blackcurrant and rhubarb & ginger.

This religious lad isn't even about the money. Sure, the profits are as sweet as the jam, but he loves making the stuff so much that that's all he focuses on. Still, it must be nice having the dough roll in doing something you love.

(The above is an excerpt from: for children how to become Rich Successful & do well in school)

In my book I focused on motivating children to learn by revealing to them that the future was bright and that even at a very young tender age – you can be Rich and successful. That all you have to do is to apply some very basic principles to your life and you can be successful. Things like: a don't give up attitude, a desire to learn, being wise and taking sound wise advice can and will help them be successful in life.

How to make extra money

Ways to make money: I could fill this book with 3,000 possible ways on how you can make more money. It would encompass the realm of viable currently working means to the far fetch exaggerated methods you easily find on the internet promising riches over night.

The truth is I can only point out some basic interesting methods and advise you to do the necessary homework in order to find what fit's you best.

Here are a few suggestions.

Turn a hobby into cash

Craft sites like Etsy and ArtFire aren't just for artists selling their work; people make money selling a wide range of products, including handmade furniture and purses. Two years ago, Dennis and Sylvia Lai of South Florida decided to turn the wedding favor they had created for their own nuptials two years earlier into an offering on Etsy and other sites. The Lais mix and design unique blends of spices and seasonings, then personalize the bottles with photos and descriptions of the bride and groom.

So far, they've brought in $7,500; not enough to quit their day jobs (yet), but "we get to express our creativity and also bring in bonus income," Dennis says. Etsy takes a cut from each sale amounting to 3.5% of the sale price; ArtFire charges sellers $12.95 per month

In some cases, you can cut out the middleman and sell from your own website. Although Jennifer James McCollum bought her first camera only five years ago, the executive director of the nonprofit Oklahomans for the Arts, in Oklahoma City, has turned her budding love of photography into a profitable side business. The $1,000 she averages each month taking commissioned photos for various organizations around the state, as well as selling note cards through her personal blog and online sales page, "has been enough to pay the monthly mortgage for the past three years," she says.

Meanwhile, the explosive popularity of e-books has made it much easier to turn prose into extra income. In 2010, Web strategist Scott McIntosh dashed off a 61-page e-book based on his knowledge of search engine optimization, then uploaded it onto the websites of Amazon for the Kindle and Barnes & Noble for the Nook. While "Google Juice" may never be a bestseller, it has netted McIntosh several thousand dollars.

Not a techie you say? Free software can be found online that will convert your Word document into all the popular e-book formats.

Invent something that can be sold and find others to invest in the idea

Crowd-fund your invention

As recently as a few years ago, inventors required bankers or venture capitalists to realize their ideas and move them to the marketplace. Now, crowd-funding sites like Kickstarter and Indiegogo allow anyone to raise money from friends and strangers who want little more than to help bring an idea to life. Of the more than 30,000 projects successfully funded on Kickstarter since its 2009 launch, the vast majority have been the work of individuals, not companies, says a Kickstarter representative. One recent project sought $250,000 to mass-produce "Impossible Instant Lab," a cool gadget that turns your digital iPhone pictures into Polaroid analog photos. Users set their phone screen onto a cradle atop the lab and press a button. The lab then spits out a picture. Contributors who pledged $149 or more received, at minimum, a discount on a limited edition Lab with free film. The largest supporters received additional freebies.

To participate on Kickstarter, you simply create an online account; write a brief description of your vision (in a few cases, like technology projects, Kickstarter requires a working prototype); decide what goodies to offer donors in exchange for their financial contributions; and designate a total dollar target. The site usually emails you within two days to let you know whether your project has met Kickstarter guidelines -- which include fitting into a category such as art, publishing, games, music, film and technology -- and has been accepted. You receive money only if you reach your goal within the specified time period, which can be from one to 60 days. Kickstarter deducts a 5% fee, but only if you hit your target. Several projects have raised more than a million dollars, but the company says the average is about $5,000. And, for many people, that can be the difference between getting their product to market and leaving the idea in a desk drawer forever.

Indiegogo is more wide open. It does not vet its projects and offers participants the option of collecting contributions even if they don't reach their targets. The fee is 4% if you reach your goal and 9% if you fall short.

One other point to consider: In September, Kickstarter ranked 348th in the country in site traffic, according to the traffic monitor Alexa.org, compared with 759th for Indiegogo, which means it offers a significantly larger donor pool for participants to tap into.

Profit from your videos

Professional filmmakers aren't the only ones who can make money from their creations, as Wayne Perry of Schenectady, N.Y., discovered last year. Like millions of other parents, Perry had filmed his newborn's first moments in 2010 and posted the results for friends and relatives to watch on YouTube. Because his newborn had grabbed hold of the doctor's instrument, Perry intriguingly titled it "Newborn baby helps doctor cut umbilical cord."

A few months later, Perry was shocked to discover that his home movie had reached 50,000 views. Last October, when it hit 750,000 (it's now 1.86 million, and growing), he signed up for Adsense and checked the box allowing commercials to run before his four-minute video. Since then, between $1,000 and $1,500 each month has been automatically deposited in his bank account. Of course, luck also plays a role: Perry has since uploaded several animal videos, but none has made even close to that amount.

Another way to profit from your videos is to sign up for the free YouTube Partner Program. In effect, this gives you your own "channel" on the site, something that may be worthwhile if you plan to upload a series of well-done works with a common theme. Humorous videos comprise four of the top five channels on YouTube, with gaming taking up the fifth. You can opt in to monetize your videos if you are the intellectual property owner, confirms YouTube spokeswoman Kate Mason, who notes that thousands of channels brought in six-figure incomes this year. In addition to allowing ads, the program offers training and mentoring to improve your video skills.

Making money is not hard, in truth – all it takes is an alert and open mind.

My personal experience: I once made $20,000 dollars in 2 months and had to patiently wait for the deal to close to collect my money. How you ask? Well, real estate was hot and things were booming, I was a Realtor at the time and I was doing well – as in averaging $3,000 dollars a month. But as I talked with investors, learned more about how contracts work and did research on how to improve my sales, I ran across some information that changed the way I thought about the whole process.

I read about how to structure deals and about a simple very much over looked contractual clause (I certainly over looked it for years) and I decided to take a calculated risk. After doing my homework I went out and put an offer on a residential lot and my offer was accepted. Using my knowledge of this clause I resold the property (*remember real estate was hot at the time) and waited for the property to close. With no money out of my pocket at the closing of the deal I was handed a certified bank check for $10,000 dollars. Overcoming my concerns and fears I did the exact same thing again the next month – in 2 months I had earned $20,000 dollars.

Sometimes, in a simplified explanation, success is simply a matter of looking, learning and doing.

"Always bear in mind that your own resolution to succeed is more important than any other one thing."
~ Abraham Lincoln

Schoolchildren know many of the details of Lincoln's inspirational life: He was born in a one-room log cabin, was largely self-educated and overcame many obstacles and setbacks.

While practicing law, Lincoln turned down several requests to supervise the studies of young would-be lawyers. He explained that he traveled too frequently to take on such a responsibility and usually added that supervision wasn't necessary.

"If you are resolutely determined to make a lawyer of yourself, the thing is more than half done already," Lincoln wrote to Isham Reavis in 1855. "It is but a small matter whether you read with anybody or not. I did not read with anyone. Get the books, and read and study them till, you understand them in their principal features; and that is the main thing."

It may be easier to succeed when we have help. A good mentor can boost our careers; money-savvy parents can instill in us sound financial habits. But the lack of those advantages doesn't need to hold us back.

You are Worth Millions
No one said 'Success' was easy

No one said 'Success' was easy – but the question is: are you up for the challenge?

I would be lying to you if I told you that things won't be difficult – but you don't have to wait until you are in dire straits before you begin to do the right things.

It seems to me that most people have the tendency, especially young people, to ignore sound advice and simply hope for the best. We all have the tendency to wait for "all hell to break loose" before we worry about planning and preparing for the very thing we allowed to happen to us in the first place.

It's like what happens to most teens with cars –they

want to drive a car, own a car and they love to drive around town in Mom or Dads car. What they forget is that a car needs gas and while they can see the car is running on empty (needle close to the big E) they still decide to put off filling the car up because it's more important for them to do something else. Which usually results in the teen being stranded on the side of the road calling Mom or dad – whomever they think will give them the least amount of flack, asking for help and saying that it's not their fault.

Like a car, success requires maintenance, it requires work. If you falter on regularly changing the oil, rotating the tires, filling up the gas tank – the car will cease, it will fail. It will leave you stranded standing on the side of the road.

You are worth millions, in your lifetime you will at minimum earn an estimated $1.2 million dollars – your job; your goal should be to work diligently to keep as much of that money as you can in your pocket. No one else can do it for you and it's something you have to choose to do continuously and with a conscious effort. Every day you will be faced with the desire to quit, to give up, to have fun (play) but if you give in to that desire, if you succumb – like a diet that many say they will start tomorrow and never do, you are only fooling yourself.

Do as I say not as I do

Thomas Jefferson wrote a letter to his granddaughter listing "A Dozen Canons of Conduct in

Life".
(Read it in the Thomas Jefferson Foundation's Monticello.org website).

In this letter we have a well known famous quote:

"Never spend your money before you have it."

Good advice which seems to go in contrary to his life when we learn that our famous third President died deeply in debt. Some of Jefferson's financial woes stemmed from his love of the good life: fine wine, books, entertaining and, of course, building and furnishing his beloved Monticello.

But much of Jefferson's debt had nothing to do with his spending. Jefferson and his wife Martha inherited considerable debt from her father. Jefferson also loaned money to others that was paid back sporadically if not at all. A financial panic in 1819 added to his woes, as banks failed, unemployment soared; factories idled and land values in many areas dropped by half. (Does it sound familiar – the recession?)

Amid all this, Jefferson wound up responsible for a $20,000 debt he'd co-signed for a friend who later died.

Perhaps more prudence in his spending would have eased his financial burdens, but like the rest of us, Jefferson was also subject to the whims of life and the economy.

Often times I find that people confuse the idea of planning and preparing with the idea of control. No one can control what will happen tomorrow just like no one can predict what will happen tomorrow, the next day or next year. But you can plan, prepare, you can control what you do, to insure a better tomorrow.

Things will happen, that is just a part of life. No one knew that in 2007 we were going to face such horrendous financial economic woes. Despite what some may say that they predicted the real estate bubble – no one knew, we all had a feeling, we were sure the party could not last forever – but we had no clue of what was waiting for us.

Things happen but you can bounce back

Christina and Jim Harris

For years, Christina and Jim Harris enjoyed a picture-perfect life. Jim's remodeling business brought in about $100,000 a year; Christina, 36, managed the company and raised their three kids, now 8, 12 and 15. Then, the recession began. It was "like falling off a cliff," Christina recalls. "Our income basically dropped by half, but we didn't cut back on expenses." By August 2008, their credit card debt stood at more than $50,000, and they found they could no longer make the minimum payments. Some people recommended bankruptcy, recalls Jim, 38, but "we decided we should pay the money back. We're not deadbeats."

"Nobody forced me to buy that $600 Coach bag," Christina says.

The credit counseling service Christina consulted got the couple's lenders to drop rates from as high as 32% to as low as 7%. The couple agreed to make one consolidated payment of $1,400 a month to the agency for four years, which the agency would then dole out to the banks.

Their spending screeched to a halt. "The year before, my kids were in all name-brand clothes," says Christina. Afterward, they were limited to one pair of designer jeans each, from eBay or a thrift store. The family did away with cable and Internet. They slashed energy bills by 20% by weatherizing doors and windows and installing programmable thermostats and energy-efficient bulbs. Instead of buying a 'new clothes dryer' for $1,200, they found the same model used for $200. They shaved $500 off their "over-the-top" holiday gift budget. Later, when they felt they could again splurge on a treat, Jim remodeled a friend's kitchen in return for frequent flyer miles to Hawaii.

Meanwhile, Christina upped the family cash flow by heading back into the workforce after six years at home. Lacking a college degree and recent experience, she took the first job she was offered, collecting bills for a doctor's office.

"I hated it," she says. She found the job so stressful that she broke out in hives at weekly staff meetings.

The $37,500 salary hardly seemed worth it, given that day care cost $900 a month, and insurance took nearly $400 more. She also felt disconnected from her kids, especially one January night in 2009 when the day care's teachers refused to let her son leave with her. "Jim always picked Cole up, so the staff didn't know me," she says. Soon after, she quit.

A few months later, when Cole started kindergarten, Christina tackled the job market again, this time more strategically. "I spent six hours a day researching employers. I wanted to find a company that treated people well," she says. To test the waters, she took a temp job doing accounts payable with a construction company. It soon turned into a full-time job managing payroll, and before long her pay rose to $45,000. "But there were no women in any power positions," she says. So in late 2011, she took a position as a project administrator overseeing regulatory compliance for another large construction firm. Her current income is "a significant increase."

In September 2012, the Harrises made their final payment, for a grand total of $66,376.07. Along the way, they established a new dynamic. "I've stopped thinking it's Jim's responsibility to support the whole family. It's mine, too, and I relish it," Christina says. By way of celebration, "I bought a Coach bag," she says. "But instead of paying $400, I got it used on eBay for $75."

Things don't always work out the way you plan

Things do not always work out as you plan, things happen, circumstances change, trouble has a way of finding you – but that doesn't mean you give up. It does not mean you surrender and simply wait to die.

Joseph Addison said it best: "If you wish to succeed in life, make perseverance your bosom friend, experience your wise counselor, caution your elder brother, and hope your guardian genius."

The reason I choose the title of this book – You are worth millions, is not because I was trying to stroke your ego. It was not an attempt to make you feel good, all warm and fuzzy. It is because you are an extraordinary person with an opportunity of a life time. You can achieve much success. You can reach great heights. You can shoot for the moon and even if you miss – you can hit a star high above. But it takes small steps, it takes time, it will take sacrifice and it will take a courageous heart.

Success is not measure in how much money you have but the achievements you have made.

You are Worth Millions

Last Word

Our worldly successes cannot be guaranteed, but our ability to achieve spiritual success is entirely up to us, thanks to the grace of God. The best advice I know to give is to give those worldly things your best but never your all – reserve the ultimate hope for the only one who can grant it.

ABOUT THE AUTHOR

Creating a better future for the young adult, author strives to motivate children and young people alike to achieve success through learning. William is a father of two children; he has spent the first fifteen years of his daughter's life and the eight years of his son's life teaching them that life starts now. That it is important to think about the future, today, even at such an early age. His daughter is a straight 'A' student and his son, is also in advance classes. They do well in school because he has taught them that doing well in school, is part of creating a successful future. It is good to dream and we all should strive to dream big dreams. But without a plan, a desire to continue to learn, to strive for more, to build a healthy confidence in one's self; it makes it that the more ever difficult to make dreams into reality.

He has written two books in dedication to his two children, a reminder to them of what can happen when you do more than just dream. The books he has written are the fulfillment of a childhood dream - a dream about being an author and publishing a book. He has taken his passion for helping his children excel in school and has accomplished one of his own childhood dreams.